Acknowledgements

To all who have contributed to the development of this project, thank you for your kindness and generosity throughout the process.

Specifically, I am extremely grateful to the following:
- To God for giving me the wonderful gift of music
- To my parents Daniel and Norma Gonzalez, for making the development of the gift possible
- To my wife Karen, for the graphic artwork and her support throughout the project
- To Mrs. John Pruitt, my first piano teacher, for her dedication to teaching piano
- And to Al Mendenhall, for his initial artwork contribution

Thank you for the part each of you played in making this project possible.

Soli Deo Gloria,

Preface

Classical Hymns for solo piano is a component of the Piano Companion series. The method books in the series provide instruction in the art of playing the piano while this book offers hymn arrangements for study and performance.

The arrangements remind us of the hymns' poetry—encouraging us in our journey. Some of the arrangements use patterns from classical piano works by Chopin and Beethoven while the remainder have been shaped by my personal musical experience. The descriptions below give the player insight into each arrangement.

- "Sweet Hour of Prayer" is a reminder of the simplicity of prayer. The arrangement includes an accompaniment pattern found in Chopin's Nocturne in D-flat, Op. 27, No. 2. The ending is a transposed quote from that nocturne.
- "Blessed Assurance" is an ongoing conversation represented by the repeating notes at the beginning and leading into the main melody—the story to tell. The arrangement has influences from Chopin's Ballade No. 2, Op. 38 in F.
- "More About Jesus" is an expression of our desire to know more about Jesus throughout the monotony of our daily lives, represented in the accompanying rhythmic pattern.
- "I Need Thee Every Hour" is a demonstration of the various ways we declare our need for Jesus—initially through a single voice, then a two-voice declaration, followed by a melody with distinct harmonies, and finally a series of rolled chords in an extreme range. All of the expressions are paired with a return to a familiar refrain.
- "Theme and Variations on Rock of Ages" is a set of variations loosely modeled on the third movement from Beethoven's Piano Sonata in E, Op. 109, and a reminder of the many ways we hide in Jesus our Rock.
- "I Am Thine, O Lord" is an expression of our desire to be closer to Jesus. Interrupting moments of agitation, represented by the repeating notes, are ultimately overcome by a peaceful declaration of our desire.
- "Praise God, from Whom All Blessings Flow" is an étude-like piece imitating Chopin's Étude Opus 25, No. 1, and a reminder of God's never-ending blessings.
- "What a Friend We Have in Jesus" is a reminder of our friendship with him as well as our need to take everything to him in prayer. It is a return to the simplicity of prayer that began with the first piece.

As you play these arrangements, my hope is that you will be encouraged to persevere fulfilling God's calling as we await Christ's return.

Soli Deo Gloria,

Contents

Sweet Hour of Prayer
(1845)

Sweet hour of prayer! sweet hour of prayer!
That calls me from a world of care,
And bids me at my Father's throne
Make all my wants and wishes known.
In seasons of distress and grief,
My soul has often found relief
And oft escaped the tempter's snare
By thy return, sweet hour of prayer!

Sweet hour of prayer! sweet hour of prayer!
The joys I feel, the bliss I share,
Of those whose anxious spirits burn
With strong desires for thy return!
With such I hasten to the place
Where God my Savior shows His face,
And gladly take my station there,
And wait for thee, sweet hour of prayer!

Sweet hour of prayer! sweet hour of prayer!
Thy wings shall my petition bear
To Him whose truth and faithfulness
Engage the waiting soul to bless.
And since He bids me seek His face,
Believe His Word and trust His grace,
I'll cast on Him my every care,
And wait for thee, sweet hour of prayer!

Sweet hour of prayer! sweet hour of prayer!
May I thy consolation share,
Till, from Mount Pisgah's lofty height,
I view my home and take my flight:
This robe of flesh I'll drop and rise
To seize the everlasting prize;
And shout, while passing through the air,
"Farewell, farewell, sweet hour of prayer!"

William W. Walford

Sweet Hour of Prayer

Original melody by William B. Bradbury

Arranged by Ruben Gonzalez

Sweet Hour of Prayer

Sweet Hour of Prayer

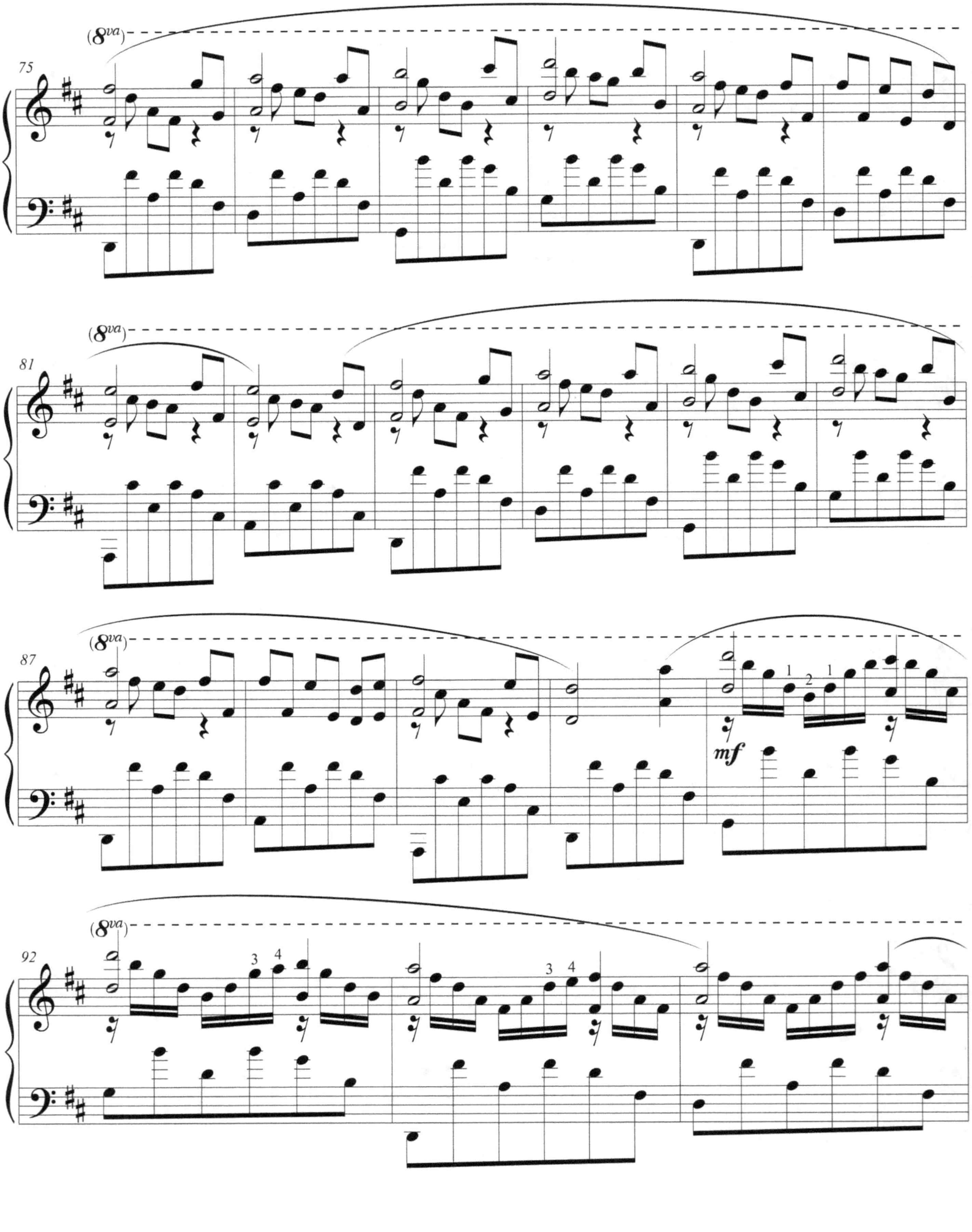
(8va)
75
(8va)
81
(8va)
87
mf
(8va)
92

Sweet Hour of Prayer

*Go to alternate ending

*Alternate Ending

Blessed Assurance
(1873)

Blessed assurance, Jesus is mine!
Oh, what a foretaste of glory divine!
Heir of salvation, purchase of God,
Born of His Spirit, washed in His blood.

Refrain
This is my story, this is my song,
Praising my Savior all the day long;
This is my story, this is my song,
Praising my Savior all the day long.

Perfect submission, perfect delight,
Visions of rapture now burst on my sight;
Angels, descending, bring from above
Echoes of mercy, whispers of love.

Perfect submission, all is at rest,
I in my Savior am happy and blest,
Watching and waiting, looking above,
Filled with His goodness, lost in His love.

Frances J. Crosby

Blessed Assurance

Original melody by Phoebe P. Knapp

Arranged by Ruben Gonzalez

Blessed Assurance

Blessed Assurance

Blessed Assurance

Blessed Assurance

More About Jesus
(1873)

More about Jesus would I know,
More of His grace to others show;
More of His saving fullness see,
More of His love Who died for me.

Refrain
More, more about Jesus,
More, more about Jesus;
More of His saving fullness see,
More of His love Who died for me.

More about Jesus let me learn,
More of His holy will discern;
Spirit of God, my teacher be,
Showing the things of Christ to me.

More about Jesus; in His Word,
Holding communion with my Lord;
Hearing His voice in every line,
Making each faithful saying mine.

More about Jesus; on His throne,
Riches in glory all His own;
More of His kingdom's sure increase;
More of His coming, Prince of Peace.

Eliza E. Hewitt

More About Jesus

Original melody by John R. Sweney

Arranged by Ruben Gonzalez

More About Jesus

More About Jesus

I Need Thee Every Hour
(1872)

I need Thee every hour, most gracious Lord;
No tender voice like Thine can peace afford.

Refrain
I need Thee, O I need Thee;
Every hour I need Thee;
O bless me now, my Savior,
I come to Thee.

I need Thee every hour, stay Thou nearby;
Temptations lose their power when Thou art nigh.

I need Thee every hour, in joy or pain;
Come quickly and abide, or life is in vain.

I need Thee every hour; teach me Thy will;
And Thy rich promises in me fulfill.

I need Thee every hour, most Holy One;
O make me Thine indeed, Thou blessed Son.

Annie S. Hawks

I Need Thee Every Hour

Original melody by Robert Lowry

Arranged by Ruben Gonzalez

I Need Thee Every Hour

I Need Thee Every Hour

Rock of Ages
(1776)

Rock of Ages, cleft for me,
Let me hide myself in Thee;
Let the water and the blood,
From Thy wounded side which flowed,
Be of sin the double cure,
Save from wrath and make me pure.

Not the labor of my hands
Can fulfill Thy law's demands;
Could my zeal no respite know,
Could my tears forever flow,
All for sin could not atone;
Thou must save, and Thou alone.

Nothing in my hand I bring,
Simply to Thy cross I cling;
Naked, come to Thee for dress;
Helpless, look to Thee for grace;
Foul, I to the fountain fly;
Wash me, Savior, or I die.

While I draw this fleeting breath,
When my eyes shall close in death,
When I rise to worlds unknown,
And behold Thee on Thy throne,
Rock of Ages, cleft for me,
Let me hide myself in Thee.

Augustus M. Toplady

Theme and Variations on Rock of Ages

Original melody by Thomas Hastings

Arranged by Ruben Gonzalez

Theme and Variations on Rock of Ages

Theme and Variations on Rock of Ages

Theme and Variations on Rock of Ages

No pedal except where marked.

Variation IV ♪ = 120

espressivo

Theme and Variations on Rock of Ages

Theme and Variations on Rock of Ages

Theme and Variations on Rock of Ages

I Am Thine, O Lord
(1875)

I am Thine, O Lord, I have heard Thy voice,
And it told Thy love to me;
But I long to rise in the arms of faith
And be closer drawn to Thee.

Refrain
Draw me nearer, nearer blessed Lord,
To the cross where Thou hast died.
Draw me nearer, nearer, nearer blessed Lord,
To Thy precious, bleeding side.

Consecrate me now to Thy service, Lord,
By the power of grace divine;
Let my soul look up with a steadfast hope,
And my will be lost in Thine.

O the pure delight of a single hour
That before Thy throne I spend,
When I kneel in prayer, and with Thee, my God
I commune as friend with friend!

There are depths of love that I cannot know
Till I cross the narrow sea;
There are heights of joy that I may not reach
Till I rest in peace with Thee.

Fanny J. Crosby

I Am Thine, O Lord

Original melody by William H. Doane

Arranged by Ruben Gonzalez

I Am Thine, O Lord

I Am Thine, O Lord

Praise God, from Whom All Blessings Flow
(1674)

Praise God, from Whom all blessings flow;
Praise Him, all creatures here below;
Praise Him above, ye heavenly host;
Praise Father, Son, and Holy Ghost.

Thomas Ken

Praise God, from Whom All Blessings Flow

Original melody by Louis Bourgeois

Arranged by Ruben Gonzalez

Use pedal throughout

Praise God, from Whom All Blessings Flow

Praise God, from Whom All Blessings Flow

Praise God, from Whom All Blessings Flow

Praise God, from Whom All Blessings Flow

What a Friend We Have in Jesus
(1855)

What a friend we have in Jesus,
All our sins and griefs to bear!
What a privilege to carry
Everything to God in prayer!
Oh, what peace we often forfeit,
Oh, what needless pain we bear,
All because we do not carry
Everything to God in prayer!

Have we trials and temptations?
Is there trouble anywhere?
We should never be discouraged—
Take it to the Lord in prayer.
Can we find a friend so faithful,
Who will all our sorrows share?
Jesus knows our every weakness;
Take it to the Lord in prayer.

Are we weak and heavy-laden,
Cumbered with a load of care?
Precious Savior, still our refuge—
Take it to the Lord in prayer.
Do thy friends despise, forsake thee?
Take it to the Lord in prayer!
In His arms He'll take and shield thee,
Thou wilt find a solace there.

Blessed Savior, Thou hast promised
Thou wilt all our burdens bear;
May we ever, Lord, be bringing
All to Thee in earnest prayer.
Soon in glory bright, unclouded,
There will be no need for prayer—
Rapture, praise, and endless worship
Will be our sweet portion there.

Joseph M. Scriven

What a Friend We Have in Jesus

Original melody by Charles C. Converse

Arranged by Ruben Gonzalez

What a Friend We Have in Jesus

What a Friend We Have in Jesus

What a Friend We Have in Jesus

What a Friend We Have in Jesus